BRAVE DISGUISES

BRAVE DISGUISES

Gray Jacobik

University of Pittsburgh Press

The publication of this book is supported by a grant from
the Pennsylvania Council on the Arts.

Published by the University of Pittsburgh Press, Pittsburgh, Pa., 15260

10 9 8 7 6 5 4 3 2 1

I S B N 0-8229-5788-4

This book is the winner of the 2001 AWP Award Series in poetry. Associated Writing
Programs, a national organization serving over 150 colleges and universities, has its
headquarters at George Mason University, Tallwood House, Mail Stop 1E3, Fairfax,
Va., 22030.

811
JACOBIK

For Flora Wilson Jacobik (1922–1984)

. . . . there is this common slate on which we merge

like lovers, on which we converge in the moment's eye.
I'm not talking to myself now, but to you: come closer,

touch me, hold me, enter me as you would your own skin
that hangs its brave disguise in the closet of words.

Maurya Simon, "Spellbound: An Alphabet"

Contents

III

I

Surréalisme

The very days and nights of Montparnasse
        must have felt mythic to those who lived them
            in that small gap between two wars,

painters and poets trying to further chance
        and let repressed desires associate freely,
            willing dreams flood each instant of waking life.

Well, they succeeded, those half-mad men fascinated
        with mystery, melancholy, and fear, for now
            we are all morphing fools, consuming

instantaneous transformation, the bizarre
        juxtapositions that come from any newspaper
            or from channel surfing, a part of everyday life.

Like them we ask more of reality than reality can sustain;
        and like them we go below, *sous,* the surface, and stoke
            the furnace of existence until it blazes ever more

vividly, each day destroying more and more of the old dream
        of an ordered life. This quest began with Freud,
            as much does that's made us so self-conscious

we sometimes find ourselves unbearable. We are like
        tightrope walkers emerging out of a maelstrom,
            the rope tethered God knows where.

Here's a matador whose hands are sharks biting the air
        as the dust of conquest settles; a printing press
            with tentacles reaching out to implant propaganda

in the masses. Contingency, indecision, displacement
in image after image; a disembodied hand pierced
by an arrow, a Corinthian column that's become

a human torso, its head a bulbous syringe. Coat hangers tumble
from a tower, become hanger-gulls that flap off
toward distant mountains. Amoebae carry flags.

Here's a seaside city of dice, a lightbulb emerging from
a bottle of light. We see it again and again in commercials,
the poured liquid that takes shape and drives away,

the violin that elongates into a rocket, this art that's taken
hold until few can imagine permanence or integrity
in anything. We expect invasion, penetration,

possession of one state by another, one entity of another,
the fluid flux of things mutating, multiplying, dissolving,
so clearly before us now, it is what we see.

Existence as Performance

Johnny Depp emerging
out of his depression is *on,*
never to be *off* until off

at last into the Irretrievable.
It is, *he is,* then, perfection,
a rather remarkable feat,

living at one remove,
all of it "terribly surreal."
Observing the one who

has grown all-too-seen,
we see how he feeds on
our gaze, while his performance

feeds us with its frightening,
and at the same time, enviable,
ongoingness. The fish in the

fishbowl who knows, who
swims to be seen swimming.
Each of his characters

becomes more real than
the rest of him: Gilbert Grape,
Edward Scissorhands,

Ichabod Crane so thoroughly
there, no one else remains.
How to wrest life back

from the cinematic surround,
from the ground of objectification,
the self as product, life as script?

The loveliest of boy/men,
of girl/women, turn into
things. But how to abound

in the birthright of pure being,
unself-consciously oneself,
the disappeared-into true

vanishing, like the unrarified
rest of us, becomes, for Depp,
a question that has too much

at stake; to avoid performance
would destroy the illusion,
to turn *off* would be fake.

Pollock's Paintings

This may be music
    moving through the night air
        looking for a Mozart,
or screaming for some as-yet   unrealized
        instrument to be invented.

Jealousy, perhaps, making its way
    toward the hand that will become
      a fist—
            or the drift
  of neurotransmitters
      moving across synapses
in search of
    the right molecules to bind with.

This could be a supernova remnant
    with its gaseous eruptions   spewing forth
particulate matter,
      pocked by antimatter,
    irradiated by gamma rays—

or anything, any force of the natural
    or preternatural world, micro- or macroscopic,
    perhaps wholly
        imagined
        and without analog,
            art creating itself.

Some say Pollock shows us chaos,
    its ubiquity,   its visual flippancies,
the liquid migrations
      of primordial stuff
as it spurts and curls and falls

through currents
too minute for us
to measure—
or the pandemonium of an entropic mind.

Nothing demonic   or divine
in this, this everywhere
and always that spells
its way through us,   or we through it.

We take his gift of motion, memory, light
that reaches out
through endless
ropes   and strings   and loops,
probes of paint
shot forth   or flung
in the dance
of human energy.

Perhaps this is Dickinson's divine insanity,
the mental traveler's dream,
the journeys of a million lives
inscribed in a lexicon of line,   color,   texture,
an infinite series of
relations graphically
displayed.

It is unfathomable, this wordlessness
finding a technique,
or as Duras says—   *As distant from words*
as the unknown object
of an objectless love—
possibilities visible in the abstract.

Meditation in Blue

A chow has a blue tongue, a soft, wide tongue that licks
the salt off you. Wittgenstein said colors are forms
of objects; what is the object blue? And when I close
my eyes I see shades from turquoise to teal to navy,

a spectrum of blues as if a sea were moving through
time-lapsed patterns of shifting light and changing
seasons. Spectral sea, invisible sea, steel-hammered sea.
Color of indefinite depths, of infinite heights, of breast

milk. The Texas bluebonnet is blue, viper's bugloss
and morning glories are blue. German *blau*, French *bleu*.
If I knew how, I'd blow you a blue kiss. *Blue Roses,*
remember, from Williams's play? No, no, it was *pleurisy.*

When Hephaestus made his great shield for Achilles,
he coated it in blue enamel, but Achilles did not drive
a blue chariot into battle. Color of illness and nobility;
her skin so pale, you can see in death she turned blue.

Veins are blue seen through skin. Larkin wrote of the "deep
blue air, that shows / Nothing, and is nowhere, and is endless . . ."
I see shades of blue when I close my eyes. The robe
of the Virgin is blue because she is The Queen of Heaven.

So sad looking out high windows on a rain-soaked field.
In the garden, Love-in-a-Mist begins bluish, fades
to silver. Muscari are blue, although called grape hyacinth.
Did you think red?—brimstone burns blue. No one's

ever grown a blue rose or a blue camellia. When Blake
saw "a heaven in a wild flower" he must have been looking
at bluebells, the way, at times, acres of them weave across
the forest and seeing them, you think: Paradise. O let

me vanish into this color when I die—it was *a blue
uncertain stumbling buzz!*—I'll come back as a blue flame
that will suggest a ghost. Rimbaud thought the color
of the vowel o was blue. How one puckers one's mouth

to say the word and then must blow the kiss of it off
the lips. Yesterday I planted blue pansies in white pots,
and I would have an all-blue garden: blue forget-me-nots
and blue delphiniums, blue daisies, blue ferns. Six blue

Milk of Magnesia bottles sit on my windowsill so
their plumbago, phthalo, cobalt can toss tiny fishes
of light across my evening wall. The shiny blue buffalo
of Thailand walk across moon-blue cobblestones

when they walk through Thai villages at night. A supernatural
blue, a perfect blue. The stones of Stonehenge are bluestones.
My favorite poem of Transtromer's is "The Blue House"
and my friend Judith painted her house blue because of it;

then she added a purple door. Windex blue, Ohio Blue
Tip Matches, varicose veins. Blue flag irises are poisonous,
still I'll have them in my garden, along with chicory
and cornflowers and bluegrass spread out like quilts

between the beds. Here's a toast to the blues of shadows,
of storm clouds, to rills in mountain streams, bluebirds
and blue jays and the blue of my daughter's eyes (the clearest
blue I know). Pale blue, almost white, dark blue, almost black.

Black hair streaked with blue highlights is the ideal. Midnight
blue hair, midnight blue love, a forbidden love, a deep
descent to degradation, the dirt and blue disgrace of it.
Chinese emperors wore blue to worship the sky, and

Massachusetts means "the blue mountains." In Paris,
le restaurant Bleu's façade is azure, its walls light blue,
blue chairs, blue tables, bluefish *la spécialité de la maison.*
I kissed you once under a very blue Cape Cod sky, June

and the water frigid, still we ran in in our jeans and
chambray shirts. I dream sometimes of rushing through
a blue snowfall, that cold escape. *The floures be small,*
the botanist John Bernard wrote, describing woody

nightshade, ". . . *consisting of five little leaves apiece*
of a perfect blew colour." Add nightshade to my blue
garden. Blue cheese. Blue night. Mood Indigo.
The blues is not a particular tune but a chorus

structure of twelve bars continually repeated,
but *Time on My Hands* is my favorite blues song,
or perhaps, *All Too Soon,* yes, oh yes, all too soon
love leaves once restlessness returns to a cold heart.

Lilies

When I bought these two days ago, I harbored
an idle hope of spirits lifted, perhaps too much to ask
of things cut from their roots and placed on a kitchen table.
They are a wonder, though, in morning light,
these Asiatic hybrids, six-petalled stars, yellow
as lemons, flung so boldly open they remind me
of a dozen water ballerinas shooting up and falling back
in plumes of kicked water as Esther Williams rises
on a central dais like Thetis ascending from Poseidon's
realm. I've put them in a tall vase; the glassblower's
added some manganese oxide for a shimmer like oil
spilled on water. Lilies that close at night, that open
themselves brazenly, green stems and leaves
between the purple glass and yellow blooms,
and above them, greenish-yellow pods. The sepals
will split apart tomorrow when the hydraulic pressure
inside each pod grows too great. They have me
asking what it takes to risk the flamboyant wildness
of a Busby Berkeley routine, extravagance so close
to excess, the dizzying heights so close to the fall?
How risk, amid a flurry of pizzicato, the long-held note?
They are extravagant without effort, throwing
streaks of shadows across themselves from petals,
leaves, and pods, swirls of bright and dark moments,
the manganese oxide adding a dozen rainbows.
But we require, to make our acts as radiant as any
flower, the transforming agent, the invisible catalyst—
spirit?—ghost?—forcing us open to chance,
to a boundlessness that strengthens as it untames us.

The 750 Hands

Mar de lagrimas (Sea of Tears)

Osvaldo Yero

Each is cast in porcelain, fired, glazed a shade
of blue or greenish-blue, some left hands,
but mostly right, and each is the hand
of a Cuban artist. Some left during
the great flight of the mid-sixties
and the lesser flights of the seventies
and eighties. And some, forced to work
in mines and cane fields, stayed in their
homeland. The hands hang a dozen deep,
a great wave on a long wall, each turned
slightly, thumb up, palm exposed.
From the side we see fingernails,
knuckles, knotted ridges of arteries,
scars of accidents and toil. Inert and cold,
signaling from stony depths, disembodied
yet overarching, as if each lived more
in the sky than in the flesh, more
in the sea than on the shore; the hands
of its people, the sky and sea that holds Cuba.
Each man or woman kept a hand in plaster
long enough to form a mold, each mold
received the poured clay, the glaze, the fire,
filling the void of absence with existence—
I lived through sorrowful times and made art
with this hand. Nothing can stop
a hand from finding whatever it needs.
Nothing can stop the maker.

Drawings: Seventeenth-Century
Dutch Landscapes

A kind of spiritual *whoosh* rings through me
    as I leave myself and enter each of these,
      caught up first by their plainspoken

titles: *Two Pigs by a Wooden Fence, Winter Scene*
    with Skaters and Hunters. A play of line
      against wash, each in a ruled rectangle,

some so small you could slide them up
    your sleeve. Modest tools—fragile paper,
      pens, ink of black or brown, chalk—

to say this was and I saw it thus. I stare
    at *Pigeons on a Chimney with a Nest of Storks*
      on the Roof of a Nearby Church. Beyond

the church, in an atmosphere just hinted at,
    a weather vane twirls its arrow-perched
      rooster, two small birds alighted for the ride.

A world that seems impossibly serene.
    Here are no larger claims, no continuities
      to rupture or mock. *Boy with Two Laden*

Donkeys in the Hills, Shepherds and Flocks
    Fording a Stream. Even the chaotic seems
      sane, the tempest restrained, a street game

of pulling-the-goose, a weak riot. Today,
    the actual cannot even represent itself,
      so shot through are we with ironic visions

and subconscious intentions. Who could
      render two beech trees, leaves turned white
      in a breeze, as cleanly as these *High Trees*

by a River with a Town in the Distance?
      A modest canal, a ditch filled with water,
         rimmed with reeds. So little to suggest

order, and that order in some way holy
      as if a divinity once permeated nature
         and left its mark on the simplest things.

The Clarinetist

On his steering wheel he taps out Cavallini's
Thirty Caprices, then sings phrases over the engine's
drone. He strains to internalize each piece
so completely, his instrument, like a phantom
coin, will disappear, leaving only the ear
and an abstract pattern. The very discipline
that makes him great makes him obsessive
and miserable. He has a long list of first dates;
perhaps his pick-up line, "What's your favorite
augmented sixth chord?" yields an unfortunate
crop. Each beginning ends because he cannot
leave well enough alone. Some days he plays
fingering charts during rehearsal breaks and
not even the upbeat Baermann melodic scales
and arpeggios cheer him. Sleep is a flourish
of notes flapping off toward night. Friends
are almost-friends who don't take his music
seriously enough. Not even a major orchestra
will give him perfection paired with absolute
control. Music without thinking of music must
exist, but how achieve it? How take from the self
what the self's been trained to do? Jean Jean,
Verdi, Mozart, the very sounds of his B-flat bass,
work against his longing to nail mastery down,
and every note he plays seems too high, too light,
never pure enough. One voice chasing two,
or interrupted, transfigured, modulated, submerged
only to reappear racier, more complex; this is the rush
he lives for: uncommon technical accomplishment
that marries theory to performance. Untempered,
his emotions stun him: there's nowhere to turn
but back to the clarinet; no life apart from playing.

Of Cos Cob in Snow

A December mist lifting from snow, the tree trunks
soaked to umber, splatters, here and there, of russet
beech leaves, lichen grey-green, grey-white snow—
the kind of morning Twachtman liked to paint.
I can step out my door and walk in it, making black
prints of boot in the melt, marking the swizzle lines
of weeping cherry, fan-like sprays of blue spruce.
I crave a Japanese sense of the delicate whole, mad
as a monk for the snowcapped heights of Fujiyama,
the lower mountain suspended in cloud, save for
three storks cutting a diagonal path. A swatch,
a swipe, a drag of the dry brush, impasto next to
the bleed-through weave of linen. An old wall drifts
left and right, dips and rises, wears a ribbon of lacy
ice. How did the painter keep his hands from freezing
as he plodded around Round Hill, worked the easel
into the muck beside Horseneck Brook? Can gloved
hands handle the brush? Americans, it was claimed,
"were formulating an impressionism minus its
violence, force, and 'virile power.'" Well enough.
It's true. Here, in Twachtman, is the pliant, the vague,
the vacuous release, as if the very breath of the year
were expiring in haze, yet how tender it looks, a place
to be lost in and buoyed by, the New England pastoral
the Pilgrims dreamt of. We take it for the save-yourself
virtues of the illumined large in a tonal range that
whispers peace. Cos Cob in snow more than a century
ago, marked by the ever-patient force that waits to move
through us again, caught as the ghost of something else.

An End of the Millennium Party

Tintoretto struts in with two plump redheads
necked under the elbows of his outstretched arms.
One woman carries a crate of persimmons, the

other a chalice of consecrated wine. Eugène
Delacroix arrives in a cart, donkey dung rounding
his soles. Braque's disheveled, as you'd

imagine, knee-torn, paint-splattered pants,
a beak-to-back John Deere cap. He swings
a ukulele and a tambourine. I've hired

caterers for this affair, requested a mixed
buffet of petites bouchées, cheese soufflés
and lamb en brochette. A bash to end

and start things with, the makers on display
(their paintings tremendously recherché).
Hopper is jaunty—springs from his Bugatti

as if bounding to the dock from his yacht,
car and yacht gifts, it's rumored, from the Met.
Well, for his vision of solitude redeemed—

or is it condemned?—by light, he's earned it.
I watch for Munch who called, delayed—
likely as not he won't make it. Oh but here's

Caravaggio, bejeweled, in amber velvet,
glad-handing his way to the bar. He feigns
a prayer for port, which I have not, declines

the pinot I offer. The night can't fail,
the right crowd's come, and here's—guess who?—
Donna Gentileschi, seductive in a midnight

sheath, politic, polite, yet she'll badger me
for contacts ere the evening's through.
The old world's dying before our very eyes.

Rubens has gained an awful lot, waddles
down the garden path splashing his martini
on the rocks. Those whose foresight flashed

the brightest have begun to fade—even
pugnacious George Bellows is mellowed-out—nods
soused in a chaise by the pool. Like a spinning

top set to whirl, the party's begun to topple.
Whatever enticed each to come out tonight
has vanished—was it one another's presence?

A vague idea of fun? The chatter's dying to
a murmurous buzz—faint-hearted repartee—
dawn's late, its crimson slashes edge into view.

II

The Shabby Truth

The Chowder House on Fisherman's Wharf in Monterey:
across the table, my grown son. I have just told him about
the second time I was raped, at twenty-eight, how it ended
my working in a massage parlor because I couldn't overcome
my fear of men after that. He shows his pain in the scowl
that rips across his face and the downcast look he keeps
a long time. The two of us are stepping across a bridge
toward one another, an abyss under the bridge. He's coming
out of the kind of fog that hugs that peninsula most mornings.
I'm walking outside of pretense as if it's a city I've lived in
all my life and never left before. I needed a lot of cash fast,
I tell him, your father deserted us—you and me and your
sister. The engine had died in my VW bus. I was too
proud to ask for help. Another scowl crosses his face,
then he steadies his gaze, takes me in, leans back in the booth.
I say this because he's just told me how he finds clients
on the Internet, knows their fantasies in detail before he
meets them. He does exactly what they want and they are
the ones in control, he says, these women who send him
a credit card so he can rent a Trans Am at the airport,
reserve a suite, pay the tab at good restaurants. One's
a rock musician who flies in from New York; another's
a plastic surgeon's wife. I am swallowing nausea with
my lemon sole and baked potato, thinking, thinking,
you will not hear me pass judgement on you, I will not
tell you about how love is impossible when money is involved,
how your soul is in peril, as mine was. Souls can be lost forever,
even in the modern world where there is no real devil, it happens.
I will not let fear creep forward, or shame steal this moment.
I was as desperate as you feel, I say, and I believed good could
come of touching people in their deepest most sacred places
even if you don't go there with them. I'm meeting their
natural needs, he says. As in giving a blow job, I don't say,

going down on an iron-bodied businessman who's between
flights at National and catches a cab to the Phase III Health
Club in Alexandria with its black walls and black floors
and ceiling mirrors, with its front room full of sleazily-dressed
women, his mother one. So I know what you must be feeling,
I say, to see these people so starved for touch they fall apart
under your hands. Yes, he says, yes, they do, they fall apart
under your hands, that's right, and then he looks up at me
astonished, wondering, I imagine, is this my mother?
There's no love in their lives, he says, nobody touches them.
It's crazy. Yes I know, I say, and look deep into his green
eyes, my eyes. We sit silent awhile, bewildered in the presence
of our truth, the presence of our lies, the said and the unsaid.

Venetian Light

Nothing could stop that car from threading its way along
that ridge-top highway, a family of seven captured and
battered by naive optimism as if it thumped its high card
down on the age's daybright casino velvet. A paucity
of humor and grams of pleasure doled out like bowls
of gruel, this was a nation of forced, false innocence
and scripted lives, 1955 and everyone feeling the gloom
no one was willing to see. When Nat King Cole sang
on TV, some said they shouldn't let him, what does
a Negro know about love? Ignorance cracks you like
a crossbeam to the back. Two parents, five children
in a Chevy station wagon, heading down the Blue Ridge
Parkway. Imagine moving across the ridge of a mountain
range in time instead of space, think of how the rises
and falls and curves of its lines might sound as the hours
pass through you. There were certain taboos on expression.
How does one catch despair sloshing like a concave
liquid under surface tension? A dirge under snappy
hit parade tunes. Dad is leading us through *99 Bottles
of Beer on the Wall* when, at eleven, the absolute
vacuity of a crushed existence blanched my field
of view. The sky began to sift down bonemeal
the way one might sift confectioner's sugar
over a cake. *Don't have children, don't ever marry,*
but of course, I silenced that voice. Leaf light flickering
from on high. Children's faces pressed against glass.
No getting out of that car except by time's midwifery.
Sputnik was not yet cruising the skies faster than any star.
Ike was about to feel the first angina constriction in his
left ventricle. It wasn't snow or ash, it was the pulverized
bones of the dead. We would stop that night in a motel,

children sleeping on pallets on the floor, a moldy stink
rising up from the carpet and orange neon slashing
our ideal bodies with venetian blades of light. Since that trip
we've traveled in seven directions in and out of this world,
racing away from each other like particles of a smashed atom,
hurrying as if the apocryphal moment had opened its mouth
and cried:

> *Run for your lives.*
> *A dragon's breath is burning your heels.*
> *The blundering world demands: Run!*

The Tapeworm

It rushes out of you the way Magritte's train engine
rushes out of a fireplace; something
illogical and fast, the long freight of embarrassing
incident coupled to fear. Groceries left at the checkout
because a roommate took your cash, a car wasting
without repairs, the dog, saved by a vet
you can't pay, so can't bring home. The ugly humiliating
chewed-up rag of it. Deadweight of trinkets
bought to console that don't console. How you can't get
enough of what you don't really want,
yet in the make-do, grab. Recompense that's supposed
to stave off—what?—the flush of shame
that stipples your neck. Two babies asleep on blankets
on a cold linoleum floor, no furniture,
no food in the fridge, none on shelves—the quick hysteria
of suppose. Suppose you borrow?
Suppose you take. . . ? But worse is the man who
promises work and delivers rape,
though he throws two twenties at you afterwards
that feed you a week. The gut-wrack of
can't-afford, primal yelp that keeps you swallowing hard.
Credit bureaus, bill collectors, taxes, bank.
The old stumble-and-fall-down, temp awhile, whore
awhile, give The Man his due. And here,
at last, you shit it out: the blind-eyed parasite who
bloodies you, the sharp-toothed gnawing
worm of desperation.

A Paradox

My youngest sister died yet did not die
and how hard it is to grieve for one
whose body, in its familiar amplitude, belies

the loss: her mind is gone. They'd classify
the accident as tragic—a truck, a red light run.
My youngest sister died yet did not die

deaf to sirens and reports that stupefied
a family huddled in a cave of crisis. A someone
whose body, in its familiar amplitude, belies

sane order. Medical shenanigans pacified
death, but not prognosis: a vegetative anyone.
My youngest sister died yet did not die.

That balm said to heal all wounds, blind-eyed
time, leaves her brain unmended. She's no one
now, whose body, in its familiar amplitude, belies

who's vanished—a woman whose wit could mollify
any ill-tempered loser. A grief I cannot run
from or empty. My sister died yet did not die,
whose body, in its familiar amplitudes, lies.

Forgetting David Weinstock

Afternoons of bed, of touch, of easy talk,
    slatted venetian light,

a bowl of floating roses on a desk.
    Copper evening radiance

on the buildings we walked past, late meals
    in outdoor cafés, the shared

carnival of city streets, all I swore I would
    remember, all

I engraved in my brain with the stylus
    of intention, is now,

for the most part, irretrievable.
    What did he say the moment

before I understood his betrayal?
    The loss is nothing to me now—

only his name sounds familiar. A heated
    argument, and later I broke

into his apartment and took back a painting
    he said I'd given him.

The Theory of Multiple Universes
    says every event is always

continuing in a world inaccessible to us,
    yet real. Each moment

of pleasure and of anguish, torrid sex
    and horrific suffering,

time and all possible variants, forever
    replayed. Does this thought

console or terrify me? An autumn afternoon.
    He hasn't yet said he loves me

but I hope he will, and I've brought a painting—
    he hangs it on the wall

opposite his bed. It's myself I want to give him.
    Slats of light through his blinds.

Blossoms of roses float in a bowl. On the tape deck
    Gould's deliberate, intense piano.

He reaches for a pack of Camels, brushes
    my breast with his arm, stops

and kisses it, nibbles at my nipple. We smile.
    He'll finish his cigarette.

We'll make love again, then go out and find
    that Italian place on M Street,

dine in the back courtyard in the warm
    October air. I make this up

because it has vanished, because it must have
    been something like this.

Perhaps there were no blinds; that detail is too
      cinematic. Maybe it wasn't October,

but April. Would he have broken off
      the stems of roses and floated

the blossoms? Only a vague quick-flickering
      montage of sensations.

This is Washington years ago, I am
      in my twenties. He thought I'd given him

the still life: a pewter cup, three eggs, a lemon,
      caught in a sharp northern light.

Night of the Great Outpouring

He woke into weeping as if weeping
had veiled the room and then the house.
She was dead set on her affairs. No one
had considered or included him. He was
outside consideration. He was outside.

But she was in another room, and he
woke her. Sorrow, that immense, hulking
cartoon shadow, had become outrage,
outrage, rage. A pounding in the stairwells
of his body, but he was too civilized to use
fists. Their past and future were arrested.

He, and then she, expelled words that,
as they whacked the other, were irrevocable.
Neither could turn back the force of such
speaking. Hope that once strode
like a queen through their lives was
now an infant thrown down a well.

Still more and more—the violations,
perpetrations, disappointments, betrayals
(large and small)—until their words became
transhistorical, no longer their marriage
alone, but their parents' marriages, grand-

parents' marriages, each union that
threw its shroud about their shoulders,
until the illimitable became limited, and
words that had been two rivers of heavy
water became transparent streams of air.

Each wept into the emptiness of the other,
into the nothing-left-unsaid, into the
not-one-grievance-held-back. Finally,
their raw and tender bodies spent, they wept
into the stillpoint that whirls like a dervish
and into the manifold passageways of sleep.

The Aftermath

You write—full of your usual jocularity, witty
as all get-out, your voice cascading down the page
telling of the soft explosions of color that are the spring,
and planning a move—*Where will I live next year?*—
anticipation almost bridal in your scampering thought.
What a deep and prolonged kiss happiness is
when it visits us once more, after a tragic year.
For weeks on end the three of us were convinced
one of us—who?—would not survive the hourly
carvings out of the heart that are divided loyalty.
You loved me; I loved you and him; he loved me.
Now this unbearably delicious goodness: each of us
at peace, restored, strengthened, and so reprieve—
who could have guessed it?—and so release—
the dove flung high, a thick thwacking of wings,
and you and I and he at ease in our lives;
the flash of agile life unfettered in the air.

The Power Outage

Still to be done, a few last Sunday night chores;
washed clothes to be folded and put away,
trash to go out. Simple doingness,
the respite of tasks. Bats are grazing fields
of air, a hoot owl calls in the back woods.
Visible from an upstairs window, the cloud-caught
glow of an end-of-summer carnival goes
suddenly black as all else. Must be children
stuck on the Ferris wheel. My palms slide down
banisters to the candle drawer. Nothing to do
but go to bed. The world is as dark as it ever was.
Wind is awash in the music of trees. We rest
in one another's arms but there's no spark
between us tonight, nothing to kindle,
so I voice a memory and you voice another,
and we go back and forth like this, surveying
in deep enclosing darkness, the turns
circumstance and promises have given us.
We seem to be drifting together everywhere
and nowhere at once, then the old impression
of eternity sneaks up, that vivid mercurial
feeling of before-and-now-and-again—and yes
love, you, and yes love, me—somehow, forever,
we're sure of it. Or perhaps this is only human,
unable as we are to imagine not being, or an end
to our love, the sense of a saving, needed haven,
when light has failed and we're in the dark.

Early October, Looking at Flowers

Isn't this pure thin light extreme
and sweet? As extreme and sweet as, to the dying,
that last look out the back of the ambulance,
family having sloughed off its objections,
and in confusion and panic had you transported
for one last circle dance with obsequious hope.

A siren needles its way through
a neighborhood, its cry fading. One day your
spirit's fair and bright and unfailing, next day
you're shattered, your ghost vanishing like
a man on a jet ski who turns into the glare—
water, light, man, a trinity of non-being.

I remember moisture pooling
on the rims of sore eyes, your lids having turned,
you'd say, to sandpaper, old age a prickly thing.
And those drab bandages on your legs, the skin
above your ankles so red and cracking I'd wince
to see it. *Skin's thin as a baby's,* you say, and grin,
as if a shimmer of pleasure existed in going out
as you'd come in.

These glorious flowers—
I've soaked up their color all summer. The cold
will have them this week or next, breaking
their stems, decapitating blossoms, cellulose
exploding on its path to rot. But, yes, this light's
extreme and sweet in its bold delay of frost,
and how much more aggrieved is human dying.

Man Sleeping on the West Coast of Ireland

On his right side, half-curled, knees high,
   left arm shielding his face, snoring lightly,
he no longer hears the buffeting winds
   toss and tumble the lays of birds, nor
the children's high-pitched calls, the baaing

of infant goats. Sunlight after two days
   of showers, and he's dull in such a deep
gathering of wool, heedless to the crashing
   surf, gull's curlicues of caws, the scuff and
scuttle of a million tourists piling in and out

of rental cars or pulling aside on narrow
   roads in car-passing pirouettes of courtesy.
The man sleeps on a bedspread, dressed,
   with socks and watch on, sleeps because
he's innocent of malice and contempt,

because he's earned this sleep, rejuvenating,
   capacious, a rest dreamt of, required. He
sleeps so deeply a winding stream could divide
   around his neck, a river's upper tributaries
collide across his chest, and still not rouse

him. Where those narcomal waters meet
   in feeder streams, in brooks, in creeks,
crosscurrents flash with bits of uneasy dreams.
   His wife, watching him three days now, impatient
to see the world they've traveled so far to see,

can almost apprehend his dreamscape, as if what
     surrounded them were not the seascape beyond
the window, but glints and flickers of a transitory
     openness that sparks and flees, possibilities dreamt
of but still unseen, a future shaping itself in sleep.

A Simple Request

Ten, at least, crows in our woods,
their clamor like bitter carping.
The hesitations that live on the tip
of my tongue. Your body bare,
caught in the slit of a bright doorway,
the wanting you then that moves in
on me like a briny wash rushing
into a spring pool. What a waste
we are, letting the least thing
stop us. Step back before all this
noise, before all its gritty erosions.
Step back so the ear can again
be the funnel the holy spirit
pours itself through to quicken
a cautious heart. Now only
insect chirr in crow-vacant air
and the inaudible coruscations
of evening clouds, a music of light.
A dalliance is what I want with you,
your body, mine, not some act
that has purpose and direction,
almost like two girls falling down
together after spinning on a lawn.
If I speak this wish, a ruby carried
a great distance under my tongue,
can you bring me to such idleness?

The Three Eyes

When I look at you with the eye of flesh
I feel a warm hand just above my pubis
and another in the middle of my back.
I see small creatures running in circles—
they race or dance—quick with pleasure.

When I look at you with the eye of mind,
I see dogwoods repeating a succession
of bud, bloom, berry—and nimble light
dividing seamlessly through a prism.
Your understanding nature rises
like a moon over a stonewhite cliff.
Your thought ruffles the kingdom of birds.

When I look at you with the eye of spirit
you begin to vanish. Words shuffle by
like miners drudging to and from work.
A sycamore drenched in the patchy brocade
of its branches is abuzz with madrigals.
And how radiant you are! What's been funneled
through fifteen billion years of starlight
are the migrations of animals, the regenerative
cycles of trees, moonrise, moonset, flight
and labor, a man who opens his arms to me.

The Frightful Allure

Mark and I talk about faith on the long, dark drive
home through the icy snowfields and tired villages
of Connecticut. He's had experiences of a numinous

presence and I envy him that, admire his telling
me that always, within days, he'd untangle
each event into a succession of possible

explanations. It takes little time to strike
meaning out of what the spirit does to the body,
what the body does to the spirit. For a moment,

his faith forms a cloud between us. I begin
to imagine a ballerina pirouetting whose
net gown swishes the air, reminding us

of the ineffable, of brushes with beauty, death.
Then the sweetness of his faith grows palpable,
and I think again of how those who know

how to live in a state of love are the ones we are
always drawn to. I watch the road for the low fox
who floats his tail on air, for the sudden deer, recall

the black bear cub run over last summer, his
midnight hump in the intersection we're crossing.
Mark struggles to say what The Good News

of the Gospel is, apart from its cultural-trappings.
The Good News is here between us, I think,
and in the dedication, commitment, promise

of our separate lives, but we agree it has to do
with compassion and agape, with the quality
of love that came into the world two thousand

years ago. I'm happy with a human account.
He's happy with a preternatural account.
However it happened, the news is still good,

glorious, in fact, and I don't mind rejoicing
in it despite my apostasy. But there's more
I can't place. In the middle of my body

the fiery charge of what was and is and will be
in motion, corporeal, galvanizing, lyrical, swift,
carrying with it, like unsecured cargo in a ship's

hold, a rolling, pitching freight—the fear of God.

Three Friends

Snow crunching underfoot, arms linked
to avoid slipping—although all might fall
in a tumble—we walk to a party a quarter

mile down the road, moon full, daylight
nearly. Frost caves the hemlocks and
the smaller pines. The air's crisp. Bursts

of snowclumps fall. A magical night,
one of us says. I'm in the middle and our
breath puffs blow out before us, three

plowing the fields of night, watching
ourselves grow older, grow more
distinctly into ourselves. In one another's

company, the insights come one step
at a time, our arms linked, stars swaddled
in moonshine, snow-lined branches spelling

dark answers, the air an insufflation,
not a sound but our footsteps. We laugh,
recalling some wild thing once said that

mattered, that changed the course of a life,
the way friends change one another's lives,
taking risks in the self-revealing litter

of exchange. I want your life to work
for you, and you, mine, and yours too,
and you mine, and thus this unstudied

wonder, friends unto the ends of our
walking this night and forward, next
year in the snow? In the squab of leaves

newfallen? Home again, the woodstove
warms us, and the cider Chris brewed
from Roxbury Russets; around us,

Margo's paintings. In the shelter of our
conjunct lives, we turn to the adventure
of each other, trust whetting the years.

Breasts

I've always enjoyed watching the jouncing breasts
of a woman walking, the easy rise and fall of flesh,
so motherly or erotic, anatomy most personal,
and yet, at times, given so freely to lover or infant,
or palpated by the inquiring hands of the physician,
flattened between the glass and steel of the x-ray,
fatty, duct-rich, nodular, capillarial, the biopsied
or augmented or reshaped, vulnerable to infection,
cyst, tumor; achingly tender at times and too
obvious or not noticeable enough, the coupled
(if she's wearing a bra) or uncoupled (if she's not)
harmonic oscillations, marked by size, firmness,
color of aureole, sign, signal, burden, shame,
always becoming old woman's dugs, striated,
bulbous, drooping downward with age, unlovely,
grotesque, nipples attenuated or inverted,
the body now barren—all this in that graceful
motion, a woman walking past, ageless, primordial,
a Lilith, Miriam, or Ruth, mother, sister, wife,
friend, an ordinary being, her breasts jouncing.

III

Angel Sex

> The sexual intercourse of the angels
> is a conflagration of the whole being.
> *Emanuel Swedenborg*

And what voyeur
could look into that fire? And how
do they wrap their wings around,
feathers overlapping feathers,
in what white dance of down?

Are they in flight
from heaven's compound eye,
disappearing through a sieve of light
as adolescents do who find a car or wood,
or pair behind the mall?

A blaze like a cymbal clash
when one angel penetrates another—in flight?
Or do they couple on the grass
or in the branches of a tree,
two ethereals ashimmer in the deliciousness
of touch, two brilliant holograms of heaven?

Does holy edict
restrict them, as the Queen of Aragon's rule
limited her married subjects to a modest,
lawful six times a day?

Lawrence saw them
transporting sperm across the phallus
of a he-whale to the womb of a she-whale,
so perhaps God's given them a role

in all coitions
and they're with us in our graceful—or awkward—
copulations, plying their luminous counterparts
as we ply fingers and tongues,
exploring, with us, sensation and response.

We climax and
for some seconds—minutes?—drift
in soft radiance. Then, as if summoned,
they withdraw, and we fall back—too quickly!—
to await once more whatever dolings-out
of transport, whatever fiery raptures
Divinity allows.

Bevy (Origin Unknown)

A company of ladies, roes, quails, or larks.
The New Oxford English Dictionary

A bevy of larks rose from the gorse
into the darkening sky, up and out
and beyond the cliffs where a bevy
of roes grazed through the evening
rousting the quails from their nests
in the heather. The bevy of quails
railed against the roes' invasion.
The larks turned back toward the land,
and in circular ascent, the bevy rose,
crying out its song as the roes strayed
closer to the edge of the cliff. A fog
enveloped the bevy of roes, who,
in the failing light stepped lightly,
yet still troubled the quails—a bevy
roo-coo-cooed long after the roes
passed. And where in all this are
the ladies?—a bevy of whom climbed
up the hillside through the heather
hoping to hear the song of the lark,
who, instead, spotted a bevy of roes
so near—too near!—the cliff's edge,
and quail running about, unsettled
for so late in the evening. Finally all
bevies turned toward bed, so that bevies
of ladies slept, and among the hillside's
gorse and heather, quails, larks, roes.

Sketch for an Elegy with Avocados and Clouds

I shouldn't write an elegy for someone I never met,
    although Larry Levis's sorrow has been
        conveyed to me and has the dappled

motley of an Appaloosa. Neither should I think about
    the man who taught me how to slice an avocado.
        First you cut it in two, hold one half in your

palm—a bright green womb—then the soft, easy slicing,
    spoon scooping the flesh from the skin.
        So sexy. So full of the sparks of touch.

Avocado trees grow in hillside orchards in Carpenteria,
    a town lovely enough for Levis's sage sorrow.
        He'd place a homeless homicidal idiot there

and raise him to surpassing glory, for Levis knew
    the happiness of truth is a cheap and dangerous
        quality. The viridian-leafed avocado trees

bow with the weight of their petulant fruit. Until now,
    my life's been a sketch, a sketch washed in pastel
        blotches breaking through charcoal lines.

The chrysanthemum light that blooms yellow
    against a whitewashed wall does not make up
        for the drear, the dread, the dropping off

at night, a Levisian despair. One applies words without
    reference, the way one bathes, or out of habit,
        like swimming laps absentmindedly,

thought finding its way back to the table on which
        the world is served. The hours flare in a carnival
        of clouds. November's done it again,

spilled the thick golden fans of the ginkgoes under
        grey streaks of sky. The year declines.
            One walks into a room that opens

onto adjacent rooms and begins progressing
        through them. I worshipped my body in 1965,
            which was, I was told by a historian

from the Library of Congress, built like a brick
        shithouse. Actually, my body was a shrine
            where I could be penitent and remain

full of remorse. You know too much for a girl
        your age, the historian would say, you know
            how to drive the rivets out of a man.

The Theory of Non-Elephants

John von Neumann

The Theory of Non-Elephants has functioned,
so far, only theoretically, although extinction,
like a train braking for its last station, draws near.

The Theory of Aspen Quaking provides much
to investigate and has applications for wind-tossed
poplars and birch. Elegant algorithms chart

the recursive paths of pollen-gathering insects.
Number crunching at high speeds lets us plot
their loop-de-loops, their general dalliance.

The variable duration of blossom-visits is a beautiful
sight graphed in three dimensions, its divergent
fractal exigencies opening out to each other the way

Norwegian fjords open onto more Norwegian fjords.
Although the applications are as yet unseen, the
Theory of Honey Gathering, like the Theory of Lichen

Disbursement, is worth exploring. Who knows
how we will need to organize ourselves when
sudden catastrophe leaves us as frantic as fire ants

whose colony has been severed by a spade?
No help yet from the Theory of Theories
with all its baroque self-reference and embrace

of existing theories. It appears to our dazed,
saturated minds like a staircase of stackable
molecules refracting the light of twelve prisms

as we climb through levels of precision and awe.
The Theory of Theories is, of course, conjectural—
creating a sequence for which there is, as yet,

no design—and this fact alone makes it tantalizing:
the patternless grand, the sublimely unstructured,
the scintillating possibilities just beyond reach.

Vet—Will Work for Food—Have Family

I pass and the lance, or laser, some incising blade,
cuts through the body politic, my holographic slice
of it. He holds the sign to his chest, a fiftyish man,
standing beside the access road to the supermarket.

That war's still warping lives—the suicides,
manic-depressives, the drugged-out, alcoholic
fringe element—vets you see/don't care to see.
High-tech firms are falsifying revenues. The

NASDAQ flares. Forensic accountants unveil
manipulations that would bedazzle any grifter,
while this—is he homeless?—neighbor, drifter,
bears/bares his bad luck broadside. My SUV

and I drive by, load up, drive back. He's still there
as the stereotypes of me he sees, and mine of him
tower in a column of virtual/actual air. All partake
of the mental media shuffle. He's in my blindspot,

then rearview, an annoying remainder/reminder,
his sign, not his suffering's what I see. No way
to dot.com his plight. He's not IPO or pre-IPO,
not marketable. An empty fuselage of a being,

I won't have him rake my yard, clean my garage,
although, in the Depression, had he come to
my grandmother's door, she'd have found a thing
or two for him to do. The State countermines

our relationship with false expectations, intervenes,
but not enough. Besides, I fear him. Suppose
he's crazy? Dangerous? A thief? Give him a
debit/credit card, sanitize/sterilize his misfortune.

Abscond, object of my callous gaze. Be rid of you. Be gone.

Unlikely Events

> An unlikely event is likely to happen because
> there are so many unlikely events that could happen.
>
> *Per Bak*

It's plausible a solar flare could touch off a series
    of intensely erotic dreams among those
    who sleep in air-conditioned houses.
And what if airtight seals suddenly began to defy
    the laws of physics—
    if gases acted like rivers?
Suppose fire ceased to radiate heat or vacuums
    began letting all sorts of debris crowd
    their spaces—or is it non-spaces?
Suppose all the unlikelihoods that wait in abeyance
    began adopting alarming propensities?
Our existence is so fragile—look around—hasn't
    the unlikely already happened? Isn't the glue
    of love that binds us one to another improbable?
And isn't laughter a strange expulsion of the breath
    accompanied by an absurd sound except
    we've always heard it?
It is unlikely I would be stringing these words together,
    one upon another, *just these,* or that you and I could
    ever believe we knew what we were thinking,
both of us constructing a unique sense of the real
    that blooms and sings and freezes and melts
    and spins around us,
doing its uncountable doings, going on and on,
    strangely marvelous, magnificently various,
    as complex as anyone's most capricious whim.

Neologisms

No word as yet in English for nature out of balance,
  any flawed detail that creates an elegant whole,
    the last fish in a kettle, compulsive cleaning,

making the familiar seem perverse. No word for
  two crows picking over carrion as a third stands
    watch. I wish there were a word for

each person's path in life and the means by which
  one discovers it; a word that catches the quality
    of what moves between us and how it

sidetracks me. A word for irrepressible desires. For two contrails
  fading into a cross. What of idle talk that reveals
    profound truths only sensitive souls can discern?

We need a word for that. A dismal bore who buttonholes
  people and tells miserable tales. Now that's a word,
    buttonholes, reminds me of *cotton,* as in "Jeb,

I don't much cotton to what you're fixing to do."
  A word for dislike that's got some teeth to it.
    A word for the politically astute and another

for those who find politics tiresome. A misguided pilgrim.
  Potentially dangerous, unredeemable statements.
    An improvement that makes matter worse—

only that word, should we find it—would devolve to cover
  many bureaucratic actions. Coin a new phrase
    and *ipso facto* it becomes *de facto,* whatever

the opposite of a neologism is. Another word we don't have.
Slang or cliché, it's a rain-soaked slope downward
to a word's oblivion. Beloved, this gentleness

that's going to end when we end needs a word,
a true name, lest it become a missing the world
won't miss, a quality vanished, a blessing lost.

Pigs on the Town

The pig was once New York's official street sweeper.
I remember this when I walk down those narrow
streets below Delancey, streets that stop, pick up

again, move in indefinite directions—old Tory
New York. I enjoy considering how Whitman
on his many jaunts might have regarded these

trotting foragers and attended to their grunting
vagaries. They slept in alleys or behind taverns
or tenements, snouts at rest near overrunning

privies or beside slaughterhouses. Early mornings
Whitman must have heard first snorts, the grunts
gathering, the hoofs clattering on cobblestones

as a pack began its dawn-to-dusk rovings.
They ransacked crates of spoiled cabbages,
bins of potato or fruit peels, knocked over

buckets of ashes and slop the night-soil men
hadn't yet collected. They were ravenous
for the tossed bones and scraps of their butchered

kin, the discarded entrails of cattle and sheep.
Peter Stuyvesant first ordered herds of swine
led through the streets as garbage removers;

by Whitman's time they'd overwhelmed
their pens and lived unmolested, although one
could spot dog-mangled ears, tails chewed by rats.

Humans would bound out of their way, troubled
not to brush trouser or skirt against a filthy
splotchy-brown hock or flank. Those whom

Deuteronomy forbad keep or eat pigs would
freeze at the sight of them. Even on Sundays
New Yorkers could gaze out the windows

of their churches and see, swilling through
graveyards, God's cleft-hoofed scavengers
defecating at will, hear them mock prayers

with guttural chortles and oinks, remote,
intractable. Whitman must have relished
how porcine nature could affront those who

put on airs, delighted in creatures blind
to ceremony, bold before carter and drayman,
deaf to fishmonger and preacher. I imagine

he floated his soul out toward them and joined
with them, especially when hogs or sows
with piglets wallowed in a mid-street mudhole.

The Lizard Man

A man has tattooed every inch of his body
with half-circular scales colored a vivid green.
Soon, no doubt, copycats—we'll find ourselves
living among creature-people, menageries
of human snails and penguins, butterflies
and great crested auks, each of us branded
decoratively as our high-affinity species.
Rather like a children's picture book where
the animals huddle round second-guessing
one who's run afoul of a farmer's rake,
we'll gossip and speculate about miscreant
breeds. Exclusive tortoise-only country clubs,
gated communities for reptilians or persons
of the bovine persuasion, we'll be species
chauvinists—for, as Heraclitus wrote,
"The ape apes find most beautiful looks
apish to non-apes." I wonder what age
we'll declare to be the age of consent, or will
we call it consecration? *I dedicate myself to the
sloe-eyed anteater . . . the bloodhound . . . the ferret . . .*
Shops, boutiques, industries, devoted to our
favorite living thing, insider gestures, ocelot argot,
off-species jokes. And then there'll be the tragic
crossings when a squirrel decides he's truly a goat,
a cougar a peacock. Tattoo transplant protocols
will be developed, but cross-species dressing,
closeted or flamboyantly exhibited in clubs,
will go unchecked. Big fuss when a gang of scarlet
ibis crash an orgy for orangutans. They'll be purists
predictably crying *cultural abuse!* when a child's raised
in a mixed species home. Yet, like the Lizard Man,
we may enjoy showing off our mottles and feathers,
splotches and stripes, scales and dapplings, and,
with panache, flaunting our etched and tinted skins.

The Cocks of the Grandfathers of Kansas

Not much spunk left in the cocks of those
    seed-sowers, those prolific propagators
of children and corn, men who once spilled
    their seed on the thighs of ginghamed girls
and the thick black soil of the plowed prairie.

A few are wild enough to try Viagra, urged on
    as they've been by Bob Dole, son of Kansas,
Republican and therefore a right-thinking man.
    Once the blood rush floods and won't
flow back, at least not for an hour or two,

what to do with the noodle so long less sociable,
    and a wife, embarrassed and dry, who
no longer contemplates the intruding member?
    But the capitalistic pressure presses on,
its capillarial action surging against the plackets

of dank Fruit-of-the-Looms, the soil of
    old age friable once more, and procreant
possibilities, while nil on the sperm-count scale,
    might yet enact some slight drama, the old man
sprung upright from his self-lifting recliner,

clopping his walker down the farmhouse hall.

Cold Constellations

I guess Mars, but it is Betelgeuse,
brightly red these nights of clear cold;
wavy skein, the Milky Way, lustrous, effuse.

Grasses crunching underfoot. The air holds
me still, slides its icy silk across my skin.
Goat, lion, ram, swan, crab, scorpion; bold

gods with sword or dagger, archer. When
the flowing lines of Aquarius spring
free from Pisces, I see Orion, then the Twins.

Yesterday, a woman in the park sang
a carol, rocking back and forth, almost
toothless, clearly derelict, no harangue

to tell the world she was mad, but utmost
mistrust, apprehension in her glance.
A cop dismounted, tied his horse to a light post,

approached her slowly, spoke. She wouldn't chance
whatever he suggested. The chestnut dropped
dung and steam rose from it, a small wispy dance.

If she hasn't found shelter by now, she's stopped
breathing. The cold strong-armed its wind across
those streets, then bitter night. In the coffee shop

I crossed to, hot, crowded, the city's lights lost
behind fogged-over glass, I remembered Irina
Ratushinskaya, the poet, how in solitary, forced

to sleep on wooden planks, forbidden sweater
or blanket, forty-six degrees inside, the scorch
of cold was the worst torture she knew in Siberia.

Of course it's fair, she carved in a cake of soap
with a matchstick, memorized, then washed
her face, *how the earth carries its damned!*

On the Irish Coast

This morning I hiked to the bog and southern cliffs.
Clouds were free-falling—long plummeting veils—
white rain over robin's egg blue. Later, I looked back
over South Harbor, arpeggios—no, archipelagoes—
of isolated grey cloudlets. How unusual to face west
toward the North Atlantic, to feel weather that's
traversed ocean and not the Great Northern Plains.
I am seeking perspective on that vast chimera
of a nation John Cage wished might "become
just another part of the world, no more, no less,"
a hodgepodge tapestry of grandeur and schmaltz,
with its aristocracy of the heart and its profound
public pettiness. Sitting on this cliff, clouds scouring
the sky, I am wrapped in my uneasy American life.
Should I stay in Ireland, I wonder?—or return
to my volatile homeland, a country that likes to
degrade and transcend itself? *Country,* an ungraspable
concept—perhaps an unleavable place. Now, near
the horizon, a thin, bluish cloudbank hovers, and
above Ballyieragh, cirrus, then mare's tails. More
joy watching sky and clouds and sea than in thinking
about a nation, yet how to weave a world at once
human and sacred, social and ahistorical?
My questions compound and spin, remain unresolved.
On this side of the Atlantic, nationality is center stage,
under the spotlight: it embarrasses me. American
without wanting to be, proud and ashamed, elevated
and disgraced, implicated in all my country does; a person
who *represents,* however ambivalently, however true.

Driving State Highway 67

> Glorious, stirring sight! The poetry of motion!
> The real way to travel!
>
> *Toad, on cars, in* The Wind in the Willows

I drive through a dozen execrable towns in south
central Texas, sun-drenched nowheres, gaudy, rough,
bracketed by 7-11s and Dairy Queens. Between them,
long stretches of an every-which-way horizon,

home to cottonmouths and rattlers, a few razorbacks
in the brush, prairie-dog hotels. Looking like obsessive
pterodactyls, all beak and wingbone, small derricks
bob and needle, extract the oil that feeds this place,

although not lavishly. No one is buying priceless
bottle openers in this part of Texas. Cattle scratch
their flanks on barbed wire leaving tufts of hide behind;
backlit, the tufts bloom like limp brown flowers.

Perhaps the cattle pick up signals from Argentina
on those resplendent horns. 106 degrees
for the sixth day running and something more
than an air-conditioned chill prickles my skin.

I'm speeding through vistas marred by an extravagant
spillage—people and their necessary/unnecessary
debris—gawking at yards of hubcap collections
and cowpoke truckers moseying out of truck stops,

holiness chapels, a nursery school housed in
a miniature Alamo. No doubt one does what one can
on any given day, same as elsewhere, but this land
lacks any beneficence, at least that I can see or feel,

not along this tar-baked highway, white-hot air
a rabid harpy on the wing, the radio a river of stale
ideas. As American as New England, Providence
having had a hand in this, too, molding a terrain

wherein humankind can multiply and survive.
Still, it's difficult to see beyond these hard edges,
one forbidding existence after another,
a minimalism writ large in a harsh and arid land.

Sweeping Sorrows

Rain last night, the first in weeks, so solace
falling asleep, leaves scraping in surges above

the wind's syncopations—the rag of the
displaced bowers. This morning, sighs from

the green, the feathered, the freshly scrubbed.
Grasses slowly upspringing. I've taken to walking

briskly, fleeing almost, as if someone pursues me—
perhaps the beggar of indolence with his

puckered mouth—the mouth of a blowfish.
There is a man I remember on rainy nights,

the smell and taste of him, the dream I had
sleeping in his arms. He was sorrow in transit,

dread on the brink of explosion, a dangerous
and exquisite creature. Once, watching him walk

toward me on a city street, I saw his immense
sorrow rise up over his body like a gryphon

merging with night's quick clouds. His
loveliness was pain, his tenderness, deception.

I love how *precipitation* straddles these lines,
as do *inundation* and *drencher,* although last

night's was simply a comforting pour. And now
down—as the direction of rain or fine soft

feathers close to a bird's skin—has entered
this poem's anteroom of unselected callers—

how many more wait for whom there is no room?
In the Sirrene's pasture, the cows are satiny,

hides steaming, flanks clean. And never again
will I see that man who would enter me

as though he were a train, such violence
and inhuman intensity, a beautiful dark cipher

of a man, now nearly vanished, no more than
a rip in the scrim of memory vexed by rain.

Ode to the Breeze

Carrier of all urges the human voice can utter.
A grace-goodness
so easily disregarded, you flip the pages
of my abandoned book,
cause me to gaze across the lake and consider
the invisible,
then, later, the breath
at my window; you skim my body's surfaces,
a space that kisses smaller spaces.
Heart-stir I feel within, without,
you are my supplest lover, and my subtlest,
finding your way under my blouse.
Time's mild marker of motion, I watch you
dry the damp bluebells,
lick the oak's crenellated fingers, turn
and swirl the nodding grasses.
Both you and the past
are beyond grasping.
Are you one or many? Ageless or as
time-dependent as a seed?
Capering spirit-mold the sculptor envies.
You turn your current over
as if it were a sleeping infant, then scissor
the air for the shiniest light, dice up the plentitude,
blue-hued governor of touch.

Considerations on a Windy Day

It is a radiant, wild June afternoon, the second day
　　　of summer, and I am observing light as it besieges
　　　　　seven windblown oaks in my yard. I am trying

not to dwell on suffering, although the Buddha,
　　　who keeps me up-to-the-minute on the enlightenment
　　　　　domain of existence, says whoever would tend me

should tend the sick. He tells me the Observer is not
　　　the same one who reasons and writes and makes
　　　　　excuses for her behavior. My neighborhood

is Paradise and my yard is a portion thereof.
　　　A blue spruce fans its dusty turquoise branches
　　　　　so violently it looks like waves crashing in air.

I've been reading E. A. Robinson's poems this afternoon,
　　　observing how he watched the folks in Tilbury Town,
　　　　　who, for the most part, cannot see themselves.

We'd call them victims of circumstance or products
　　　of deficient family constellations, but he has
　　　　　a compassionate regard for them, which might

be the best any creator can do. Contingency, circumstance,
　　　character, the three big abstractions that govern fate.
　　　　　This is a day of light and clouds creating contrasts,

when weather conditions lend themselves to observations
　　　rich and manifold in their complexity. How is
　　　　　equilibrium ever achieved amid so much change?

The wind keeps the flies and mosquitoes blowing past me,
and forms a flickering swirl of ferns in shifting
light. Great beauty and great suffering

bewilder us. The Observer has no access to words
or feelings, and gender and other marks of identity
are beyond its ken. You will have to ask

the Buddha to explain how thought is thinking this,
for I have fallen back into my hard-driving
personality and lost all perspective.

Beauty's Embrace

The Universe is accelerating in its expansion.
We can suppose this fortunate or not, but no one knows.
Perhaps the end of time is a supersymmetric equation
knocking on someone's brain. Like any unrealized event,
it seeks expression. Mathematics and physics—neither's shown
an interest in my intelligence, yet here I am listening to rain,
its everywhere-at-once patter, its scattershot drone
like the radiation flung onto the surface of last scattering,
when elation sidles up like a cat, familiar, fickle, ever lovely;
elation, who writes her own rules. I say *her* because that's
the way she comes to me, although of course, she's genderless,
as is the Universe, as is the idea of expansion. It's raining
and it's evening. I've been reading a book on cosmology.
Right of the book, a lit candle, left, a vase of zinnias, mostly red.
Only the silent inexpressible expansion of words and rain falling.
The beauty of the world is enough to annihilate anyone
who opens the aperture of spirit fully. You die into beauty
as if you'd fallen headlong into a lake flickering with silver light.
Later, floating on your back, barn swallows drape swags of flight
that ray in all directions from your body. There's a dozen notes
for this near the end of Mahler's *Resurrection Symphony*.
The center of the Universe is at once the center of your soul.
We never know what's going to happen next. You may
encounter the word *aperspectival* or *holonographic* and something
shifts forever. Rain intensifies, streamlets begin adding
trickling sounds that carillon through grass. A car whisks by
on the grid that plots the curvature of space. Tonight
I'll sleep in the embrace of a unifying principle. It will
lull my ego into letting go its clamp on freedom. My spirit
will expand into succoring night, deepest night into dawn.

Notes

The epigraph from "Spellbound: An Alphabet" by Maurya Simon was published in *Speaking in Tongues,* Peregrine Smith Books, Salt Lake City, Utah, 1990.

The quote from Marguerite Duras at the end of "Pollock's Paintings" comes from her book *Writing* translated by Mark Polizzotti, Lumen Editions, Cambridge, Mass., 1998.

Many of the facts that I've woven into "Meditation in Blue" I found in Alexander Theroux's essay on blue in his book *The Primary Colors;* Henry Holt and Company, Inc., 1994.

In "The Clarinetist," the line, "What's your favorite augmented sixth chord?" is taken from a website called The Music Geek, http://www.clarinet.org/musicgeek .htm.

The quote in "Of Cos Cob in Snow" comes from Kathleen A. Pyne's essay "John Twachtman and The Therapeutic Landscape" printed in *John Twachtman: Connecticut Landscapes,* published by the National Gallery of Art, Washington, D.C., 1989. Pyne takes the phrase "impressionism minus its violence" from an 1896 review of J. Alden Weir's work in the *Boston Transcript.*

"Three Friends" is dedicated to my dear friends, Margo Giroux and Chris Holt.

Regarding the Queen of Aragon's six times a day limit ("Angel Sex"), Montaigne, in his *Essays,* wrote the following about the Queen of Aragon: "After mature deliberation of counsel, the good Queen to establish a rule and imitable example unto all posterity, for the moderation and required modesty in a lawful marriage, ordained the number of six times a day as a lawful, necessary and competent limit."

"The Theory of Non-Elephants" and "Unlikely Events": According to Per Bak (*How Nature Works,* Copernicus, 1996), "The legendary Hungarian mathematician John von Neumann once referred to the theory of nonequilibrium systems as the 'theory of non-elephants,' that is, there can be no unique theory of this vast area of science."

"Neologisms": Some of the ideas for words that do not exist derive from ideas presented in Howard Rheingold's book, *They Have a Word For It: A Lighthearted Lexicon of Untranslatable Words & Phrases,* Sarabande Books, Louisville, Kentucky, 2000.

"Pigs on the Town": I first learned about the scavenger pigs of nineteenth-century Manhattan from reading *Paddy's Lament* by Thomas Gallagher, Harcourt Brace, 1982.

The quote from Heraclitus in "The Lizard Man" is fragment XCIX as translated by Brooks Haxton and published in *Fragments: The Collected Wisdom of Heraclitus,* Penguin Putnam, Inc.

"The Cocks of the Grandfathers of Kansas": The title of this poem comes from a phrase in Allen Ginsberg's "Footnote to Howl."

The quote from Irina Ratushinskaya in "Cold Constellations" can be found in her book *Beyond the Limit,* translated by Frances Padoor Brent and Carol J. Avins, Northwestern University Press, 1987. In the forward, writing about Ratushinskaya's imprisonment in 1983 at Barashevo, a prison camp in the Soviet Dubrovlag network, Brent writes, "It was in the solitude of *shizo* that most of her poems from *Beyond the Limit* were written with a sharpened matchstick on a bar of soap. When they were memorized, the poet washed her hands and the palimpsest was erased."

The quote in "On the Irish Coast" can be found in John Cage's *A Year from Monday* and in his *M: writings '67–'72.*

Acknowledgments

The author wishes to express grateful acknowledgment to the following publications in which these poems (some in earlier versions or with different titles) first appeared: *American Literary Review* ("Unlikely Events"); *Antioch Review* ("Surréalisme"); *Connecticut Review* ("Cold Constellations," "Driving Highway 67," "Vet—Have Family—Will Work for Food"); *Diner* ("Of Cos Cob in Snow," "Lilies," "Night of the Great Outpouring," "The Shabby Truth," "The Theory of Non-Elephants"); *Image: A Journal of the Arts and Religion* ("The Frightful Allure"); *Iron Horse Literary Review* ("Sweeping Sorrows"); *Ontario Review* ("Forgetting David Weinstock"); *Poet Lore* ("The 750 Hands"); *Poetry* ("Pollock's Paintings"); *The Recorder: The Journal of the American Irish Historical Society* ("On the Irish Coast"); *The Salt River Review* ("The Power Outage" and "The Tapeworm").

"The Shabby Truth" received the 1997 Yeats Prize awarded by the Yeats Society of New York.

I wish to express my deep gratitude toward three remarkable poets who read this work in manuscript and offered suggestions that have improved it: Robert Cording, Maurya Simon and Mary Ann Larkin. Members of The Brickwalk Poets read each poem as I created it, always offering honest responses and thoughtful criticisms that shaped final versions. I am fortunate to read and write among so many fine poets: Charles Chase, Marilyn Johnston, Paula Adams Nelson, Anne Sheffield, Susan Finnegan, Connie Voisine, Brad Davis, Maria Sassi, James Finnegan, Clare Rossini, and Jeff Mock. Deborah Meade of the University of Pittsburgh Press, through her extraordinary editing, made a significant contribution to the quality of this book. My first and most sagacious reader is my husband, Bruce Gregory, whose ability to see what must not stay permits me to see what remains.

Gray Jacobik is the author of *The Surface of Last Scattering,* which won the X. J. Kennedy Poetry Prize, *The Double Task,* winner of the Juniper Prize, *Sandpainting, Paradise Poems,* and *Jane's Song.* Widely published in literary magazines and journals, Jacobik has been the recipient of a National Endowment for the Arts Fellowship, an Artist's Fellowship from the Connecticut Commission on the Arts, the Yeats Prize, and the Emily Dickinson Prize. She is a member of the English faculty at Eastern Connecticut State University.